christmas

simple and delicious easy-to-make recipes

Mavis Young

This is a Parragon Publishing Book
This edition published in 2003

Parragon Publishing
Queen Street House
4 Queen Street
Bath, BA1 1HE, UK

ISBN: 1-40541-519-3

Printed in China

Produced by the Bridgewater Book Company Ltd.

Photographer Calvey Taylor-Haw

Home Economist Ruth Pollock

Cover by 20 Twenty Design

NOTES FOR THE READER

- This book uses both imperial and metric measurements. Follow the same units of measurement throughout; do not mix imperial and metric.

- All spoon measurements are level: teaspoons are assumed to be 5 ml, and tablespoons are assumed to be 15 ml.

- Unless otherwise stated, milk is assumed to be whole milk, eggs and individual vegetables such as carrots are medium, and pepper is freshly ground black pepper.

- Recipes using raw eggs should be avoided by infants, the elderly, pregnant women, convalescents, and anyone suffering from an illness.

- The times given are an approximate guide only. Preparation times differ according to the techniques used by different people and the cooking times may also vary from those given. Optional ingredients, variations, or serving suggestions have not been included in the calculations.

contents

Introduction

Enjoying delicious food is an intrinsic part of Christmas. Where would we be without the seasonal delights of succulent turkey and cranberries, sweet mince pies, rich Christmas pudding and luscious brandy butter? And who could imagine festivities without the party cheer of Christmas punch and the sweet spices of mulled wine?

This book features a dazzling array of festive recipes that will conjure up the cheer of the season wherever you happen to be. You'll find many traditional favorites here, such as roast turkey, Christmas pudding, mince pies, and a sherry trifle. There are also contemporary and international dishes, such as Roast Turkey Oriental-Style and Mozzarella Crostini with Pesto & Caviar. Vegetarians will enjoy the Feta Cheese & Cranberry Tarts and the Mixed Nut Roast with Cranberry & Red Wine Sauce.

Christmas is a time for truly mouthwatering fare, whether you are entertaining a large group of people or curling up with homemade treats in front of a crackling fire. So wherever you will be this Christmas, and whatever you are planning to do, there will be something here to suit the occasion.

guide to recipe key		
	very easy	Recipes are graded as follows: 1 pea = easy; 2 peas = very easy; 3 peas = extremely easy.
	serves 4	Recipes generally serve four people. Simply halve the ingredients to serve two, taking care not to mix imperial and metric measurements.
	10 minutes	Preparation time. Where marinating, chilling, or cooling are involved, these times have been added on separately: eg, 15 minutes + 30 minutes to marinate.
	10 minutes	Cooking time. Cooking times don't include the cooking of side dishes or accompaniments served with the main dishes.

salmon tartare
page 18

roast garlic potatoes
page 34

yuletide goose with honey & pears
page 54

white chocolate truffles
page 88

soups
& appetizers

Start your Christmas meal off with a swing with this magnificent array of soups and appetizers. In this chapter, tantalizing combinations of flavors, such as wild mushrooms with sherry, and turkey and leek with tarragon, make irresistible soups you will want to savor again and again. If you are entertaining a group of people, why not impress them with a truly elegant appetizer, such as the Salmon Tartare or the Chèvre & Oyster Tartlets? Whatever you choose, these dishes will delight everyone and leave them longing for more.

wild mushroom & sherry soup

		ingredients	
	very easy	2 tbsp olive oil	5½ oz/150 g wild mushrooms
		1 onion, chopped	2½ cups vegetable bouillon
	serves 4	1 garlic clove, chopped	1½ cups light cream
		4½ oz/125 g sweet potato, peeled	4 tbsp sherry
		and chopped	salt and pepper
	15 minutes	1 leek, trimmed and sliced	
		7 oz/200 g white and crimini	TO GARNISH
		mushrooms	Parmesan shavings
			sautéed wild mushrooms, sliced
	35 minutes		fresh crusty rolls, to serve

Heat the oil in a pan over medium heat. Add the onion and garlic and cook, stirring, for 3 minutes until softened slightly. Add the sweet potato and cook for another 3 minutes. Stir in the leek and cook for another 2 minutes.

Stir in the mushrooms, bouillon, and cream. Bring the mixture to a boil, then reduce the heat and simmer gently, stirring occasionally, for about 25 minutes. Remove from the heat, stir in the sherry, and let cool a little.

Transfer half of the soup into a food processor and blend until smooth. Return the mixture to the pan with the rest of the soup, season with salt and pepper and reheat gently, stirring. Pour into 4 warm soup bowls, garnish with Parmesan shavings and wild mushrooms, and serve with fresh crusty rolls.

turkey, leek & stilton soup

		ingredients	
very easy		4 tbsp butter	$^2/_3$ cup heavy cream
		1 large onion, chopped	1 tbsp chopped fresh tarragon
serves 4		1 leek, trimmed and sliced	pepper
		11$^1/_2$ oz/325 g cooked turkey	
		meat, sliced	GARNISH
		2$^1/_2$ cups chicken bouillon	fresh tarragon leaves
15 minutes		5$^1/_2$ oz/150 g Stilton or other strong	croûtons
		blue cheese	
25 minutes			

Melt the butter in a pan over medium heat. Add the onion and cook, stirring, for 4 minutes, until slightly softened. Add the leek and cook for another 3 minutes.

Add the turkey to the pan and pour in the bouillon. Bring to a boil, then reduce the heat and simmer gently, stirring occasionally, for about 15 minutes. Remove from the heat and let cool a little.

Transfer half of the soup into a food processor and blend until smooth. Return the mixture to the pan with the rest of the soup, stir in the Stilton, cream, and tarragon, and season with pepper. Reheat gently, stirring. Remove from the heat, pour into 4 warm soup bowls, garnish with tarragon and croûtons, and serve.

spiced pumpkin soup

		ingredients	
very easy		2 tbsp olive oil	1 bay leaf
		1 onion, chopped	2 lb 4 oz/1 kg pumpkin, peeled,
serves 4		1 garlic clove, chopped	seeded, and diced
		1 tbsp chopped fresh gingerroot	2½ cups vegetable bouillon
		1 small red chile, seeded and	salt and pepper
15 minutes		finely chopped	light cream, to garnish
		2 tbsp chopped fresh cilantro	
35 minutes			

Heat the oil in a pan over medium heat. Add the onion and garlic and cook, stirring, for about 4 minutes, until slightly softened. Add the gingerroot, chile, cilantro, bay leaf, and pumpkin, and cook for another 3 minutes.

Pour in the bouillon and bring to a boil. Using a perforated spoon, skim any scum from the surface. Reduce the heat and simmer gently, stirring occasionally, for about 25 minutes, or until the pumpkin is tender. Remove from the heat, take out the bay leaf, and let cool a little.

Transfer the soup into a food processor and blend until smooth (you may have to do this in batches). Return the mixture to the pan and season with salt and pepper. Reheat gently, stirring. Remove from the heat, pour into 4 warm soup bowls, garnish each one with a swirl of cream, and serve.

mozzarella crostini
with pesto & caviar

ingredients

very easy	
serves 4	
20 minutes	
15 minutes	

8 slices white bread, crusts removed
3 tbsp olive oil
7 oz/200 g mozzarella, cut into
  thin pieces
6 tbsp lumpfish caviar

PESTO
1¼ cups finely chopped fresh basil
¼ cup pine nuts, finely chopped
2 garlic cloves, finely chopped
3 tbsp olive oil

Preheat the oven to 350°F/180°C. Using a sharp knife, cut the bread into fancy shapes, such as half-moons, stars, and Christmas trees. Drizzle with oil, transfer to an ovenproof dish, and cook in the preheated oven for 15 minutes.

While the bread is cooking, make the pesto. Put the basil, pine nuts, and garlic into a small bowl. Pour in the olive oil and stir together well.

Remove the bread shapes from the oven and let cool. Spread a layer of pesto on the shapes, top each one with a piece of mozzarella and some caviar, and serve.

olive tapenade toasts

		ingredients	
very easy	1 large baguette (preferably 1 day old), cut into slices	TAPENADE	
	2 tbsp olive oil	generous 1 cup black olives, pitted	
serves 4		3 canned anchovy fillets, drained	
		1 garlic clove, chopped	
		2 tbsp blanched almonds, chopped	
15 minutes		4 tbsp olive oil	
		1 tsp lemon juice	
15 minutes		salt and pepper	

Preheat the oven to 350°F/180°C. Spread the baguette slices with oil, put them into an ovenproof dish, and cook in the preheated oven for 15 minutes.

While the bread is cooking, make the tapenade. Put the olives, anchovies, garlic, and almonds into a food processor and blend until combined. With the motor running, slowly pour in the olive oil through the feed tube, then add the lemon juice. Season with salt and pepper and transfer to a bowl. Cover with plastic wrap and refrigerate until needed.

Remove the bread shapes from the oven and let cool. Spread each piece with tapenade and serve.

salmon tartare

	very easy	**ingredients**

ingredients

1lb 2 oz/500 g salmon fillet, skin removed	TOPPING
2 tbsp sea salt	1¾ cups cream cheese
1 tbsp superfine sugar	1 tbsp chopped fresh chives
2 tbsp chopped fresh dill	pinch of paprika
pepper	sprigs of fresh dill, to garnish
1 tbsp chopped fresh tarragon	
1 tsp Dijon mustard	
juice of 1 lemon	

very easy

serves 4

20 minutes + 48 hours to marinate

—

Put the salmon into a shallow glass dish. Combine the sea salt, sugar, and dill, then rub the mixture into the fish until well coated. Season the salmon with plenty of pepper. Cover with plastic wrap and refrigerate for at least 48 hours, turning once.

When ready to serve, put the chopped tarragon into a mixing bowl with the mustard and lemon juice. Season well. Remove the salmon from the refrigerator, chop into small pieces, then add to the bowl. Stir until the salmon is well coated.

To make the topping, put the cream cheese, chives, and paprika into a separate bowl and mix well. Place a 4-inch/10-cm steel cooking ring or circular cookie cutter on each of 4 small serving plates. Divide the salmon between the four steel rings so that each ring is half-full. Level the surface of each one, then top with the cream cheese mixture. Smooth the surfaces, then carefully remove the steel rings. Garnish with sprigs of fresh dill and serve.

chèvre & oyster tartlets

		ingredients	
	very easy	scant 1 cup all-purpose flour, plus extra	1 onion, chopped
		for dusting	12 oysters, cleaned
	makes 12	pinch of salt	2 tbsp chopped fresh parsley
		3½ oz/100 g butter, chopped, plus	salt and pepper
		extra for greasing	7 oz/200 g goat cheese, crumbled
	20 minutes + 45 minutes to chill	1 egg yolk	sprigs of fresh flatleaf parsley, to garnish
	20 minutes		

Strain the flour and salt together in a bowl. Rub in all but 1 tablespoon of the butter, then mix in the egg yolk to make a dough. Add a little cold water if needed. Shape into a ball and turn out onto a lightly floured counter. Roll out to a thickness of ¼ inch/5mm. Grease 12 small tartlet pans, about 2¾ inches/7 cm in diameter, with butter. Line them with dough and trim the edges, then chill for 45 minutes to prevent the pastry shrinking.

Preheat the oven to 400°F/200°C. Bake the tartlet shells for 10 minutes until golden. Meanwhile, heat the remaining butter in a pan over medium heat, add the onion, and cook for 4 minutes, stirring. Take the oysters out of their shells, add to the pan with the parsley, season, and cook for 1 minute. Remove the tartlets from the oven. Divide 3½ oz/100 g of the goat cheese between them. Top with the oyster mixture, crumble over the remaining cheese, then bake for 10 minutes. Garnish with fresh parsley and serve hot.

light meals, snacks & side dishes

Christmas is not always just one big feast, but rather a series of special meals over several days. When lighter meals are required, what better way to keep the spirit of Christmas going than with a selection of festive snacks? This chapter contains some delicious mini-feasts, such as Turkey Tortillas with Sour Cream, which provide a practical way of using any leftover turkey. The chapter finishes with a tempting selection of vegetable accompaniments that will prove a tasty addition to the Christmas meal or to any light supper.

spiced apple, brie
& arugula salad

		ingredients	
very easy		generous 2 cups red wine	DRESSING
		½ cup sugar	3 tbsp red wine vinegar
serves 4		1 cinnamon stick	½ cup extra-virgin olive oil
		1 tbsp grated fresh gingerroot	1 tbsp honey
		4 large apples	
		2 tbsp lemon juice	
15 minutes		5½ oz/150 g arugula leaves	
		5½ oz/150 g Brie, cubed	
		salt and pepper	
20 minutes			

Put the wine, sugar, cinnamon, and gingerroot into a large pan and bring to a boil. Reduce the heat and simmer gently for 10 minutes. Core and slice the apples, and brush with lemon juice. Add the apple slices to the pan and cook for another 10 minutes. Remove from the heat and let cool completely.

To make the dressing, put the vinegar, olive oil, and honey into a glass jar, screw on the lid, and shake well. Alternatively, put the ingredients into a small bowl and whisk together.

To assemble the salad, put the arugula leaves into a salad bowl. Drain the apples well and scatter them over the arugula, then top with Brie and season with salt and pepper. Drizzle over the dressing, toss the salad until well coated, and serve.

monkfish parcels

		ingredients	
very easy		4 tsp olive oil	6 strips smoked lean bacon
		2 zucchini, trimmed and sliced	salt and pepper
serves 4		1 large red bell pepper, skinned, seeded, and cut into strips	TO SERVE
		2 monkfish fillets, about 4½ oz/125 g each, skin and membrane removed	freshly cooked pasta
15 minutes			slices of fresh olive bread
25 minutes			

Preheat the oven to 375°F/190°C. Cut out 4 large pieces of foil, about 9 inches/23 cm square. Brush them lightly with oil, then divide the zucchini and bell pepper between them.

Rinse the fish fillets under cold running water and pat dry with paper towels. Cut them in half, then place one piece on top of each pile of zucchini and bell pepper. Cut the bacon strips in half, and lay 3 pieces across each piece of fish. Season with salt and pepper, drizzle over the remaining oil, and close up the parcels. Seal tightly, transfer to an ovenproof dish, and bake in the preheated oven for 25 minutes.

Remove from the oven, open each foil parcel slightly, and serve with freshly cooked pasta and slices of fresh olive bread.

turkey tortillas
with sour cream

		ingredients	

very easy	1 tbsp olive oil
	1 onion, chopped
	1 garlic clove, chopped
	1 zucchini, trimmed and sliced
	2 tomatoes, sliced
	1 small red chile, seeded and
	  finely chopped
		1 tbsp red wine
		8 flour tortillas, warmed
		12 oz/350 g cooked turkey meat,
		  shredded
		$\frac{1}{2}$ cup sour cream
		
		fresh salad greens, to garnish
		
		crusty whole-wheat rolls, to serve

serves 4			
10 minutes			
10 minutes			

Heat the oil in a skillet over medium heat. Add the onion, garlic, and zucchini and cook, stirring, for 4 minutes. Add the tomatoes, chile, and red wine, cook for another 5 minutes, then remove from the heat.

Arrange the warmed tortillas on a clean counter and spoon some tomato and zucchini mixture onto each one. Add some shredded turkey and a spoonful of sour cream, then roll up the tortillas and arrange them on serving plates. Garnish with salad greens and serve with crusty whole-wheat rolls.

honeyed parsnips

		ingredients
	very easy	8 parsnips, peeled and cut into fourths
		4 tbsp vegetable oil
	serves 4	1 tbsp honey
	5 minutes	
	50 minutes	

Preheat the oven to 350°F/180°C.

Bring a large pan of water to a boil. Reduce the heat, add the parsnips, and cook for 5 minutes. Drain thoroughly.

Pour 2 tablespoons of the oil into a shallow, ovenproof dish and add the parsnips. Mix the remaining oil with the honey and drizzle over the parsnips. Roast in the preheated oven for 45 minutes until golden brown and tender. Remove from the oven and serve.

spiced winter vegetables

		ingredients	
very easy		2 large baking potatoes, scrubbed but left unpeeled	1 garlic clove, finely chopped
serves 4		2 parsnips, scrubbed and trimmed but left unpeeled	6 tbsp chili oil or extra-virgin olive oil
15 minutes		4 large carrots	$\frac{1}{2}$ tsp mild chili powder
1 hour 10 minutes			pinch of paprika
			salt and pepper

Preheat the oven to 425°F/220°C. Bring a pan of water to a boil.

Cut the potatoes and parsnips into wedges. Cut the carrots lengthwise and then diagonally into large pieces of a similar size to the potato and parsnip wedges. Add the vegetables to the pan and cook for 10 minutes. Drain thoroughly and let cool.

Put the garlic, oil, chili powder, and paprika into a pitcher or small bowl and mix together well. Transfer the vegetables to an ovenproof dish and pour over the oil mixture. Season with salt and pepper. Turn the vegetables in the oil until thoroughly coated. Roast in the preheated oven for at least 1 hour, or until golden brown and tender. Remove from the oven and serve.

roast garlic potatoes

		ingredients	
	very easy	1 lb 5 oz/600 g small new potatoes, scrubbed	½ tsp salt
			pinch of paprika
	serves 4	2 garlic cloves, chopped	pepper
		3 tbsp olive oil	
	10 minutes		
	50 minutes		

Preheat the oven to 400°F/200°C. Arrange the potatoes in a roasting pan.

Put the garlic into a small pitcher or bowl. Add the oil, salt, paprika, and pepper and mix together well. Pour the oil mixture over the potatoes, then turn the potatoes in the mixture until thoroughly coated. Roast in the preheated oven for 50 minutes, basting occasionally, until golden brown and tender. Remove from the oven and serve.

honey-glazed red cabbage
with golden raisins

		ingredients	
very easy		2 tbsp butter	1 tbsp honey
		1 garlic clove, chopped	scant $\frac{1}{2}$ cup red wine
serves 4		1 lb 7 oz/650 g red cabbage, shredded	scant $\frac{1}{2}$ cup water
		scant 1 cup golden raisins	
10 minutes			
50 minutes			

Melt the butter in a large pan over medium heat. Add the garlic and cook, stirring, for 1 minute, until slightly softened.

Add the cabbage and golden raisins, then stir in the honey. Cook for another minute. Pour in the wine and water and bring to a boil. Reduce the heat, cover, and simmer, stirring occasionally, for about 45 minutes, or until the cabbage is cooked. Serve hot.

brussels sprouts
with buttered chestnuts

very easy	**ingredients**
serves 4	12 oz/350 g Brussels sprouts, trimmed ½ cup slivered almonds, to garnish 3 tbsp butter 3½ oz/100 g canned whole chestnuts pinch of nutmeg salt and pepper
10 minutes	
10 minutes	

Bring a large pan of salted water to a boil. Add the Brussels sprouts and cook for 5 minutes. Drain thoroughly.

Melt the butter in a large pan over medium heat. Add the Brussels sprouts and cook, stirring, for 3 minutes, then add the chestnuts and nutmeg. Season with salt and pepper and stir well. Cook for another 2 minutes, stirring, then remove from the heat. Transfer to a serving dish, scatter over the almonds, and serve.

garlic mushrooms with
white wine & chestnuts

		ingredients	
very easy		4 tbsp butter	salt and pepper
		4 garlic cloves, chopped	10½ oz/300 g canned whole chestnuts
serves 4		7 oz/200 g white mushrooms, sliced	3½ oz/100 g chanterelle mushrooms,
		7 oz/200 g crimini mushrooms, sliced	sliced
		4 tbsp dry white wine	
15 minutes		scant ½ cup heavy cream	chopped fresh parsley, to garnish
10 minutes			

Melt the butter in a large pan over medium heat. Add the garlic and cook, stirring, for 3 minutes, until softened. Add the white and crimini mushrooms and cook for another 3 minutes.

Stir in the wine and cream and season with salt and pepper. Cook for 2 minutes, stirring, then add the chestnuts and the chanterelle mushrooms. Cook for another 2 minutes, stirring, then remove from the heat and transfer to a serving dish. Garnish with chopped fresh parsley and serve.

entrées

Transform your Christmas meal into a
veritable banquet with the stunning display
of dishes in this chapter. From Roast Turkey,
Yuletide Goose, and succulent Duck with
Blueberries to Redcurrant-Glazed Ham and a
mouthwatering selection of sauces, there is
something to tempt everyone. The Herbed
Salmon with Hollandaise Sauce will delight
fish-lovers, and delicious, meat-free recipes
such as a festive Nut Roast and Feta Cheese
& Cranberry Tarts will have the vegetarians
among you coming back for more.

mixed nut roast with
cranberry & red wine sauce

		ingredients	
easy		2 tbsp butter, plus extra for greasing	salt and pepper
		2 garlic cloves, chopped	
serves 4		1 large onion, chopped	CRANBERRY & RED WINE SAUCE
		$\frac{1}{2}$ cup hazelnuts, toasted and ground	$1\frac{3}{4}$ cups fresh cranberries
		$\frac{1}{2}$ cup walnuts, ground	$\frac{1}{2}$ cup superfine sugar
		$\frac{1}{3}$ cup cashews, ground	$1\frac{1}{4}$ cups red wine
30 minutes		$\frac{1}{2}$ cup pine nuts, toasted and ground	1 cinnamon stick
		scant 2 cups whole-wheat bread crumbs	sprigs of fresh thyme, to garnish
		1 egg, lightly beaten	Brussels Sprouts with Buttered
35 minutes		2 tbsp chopped fresh thyme	Chestnuts (see page 38), to serve
		1 cup vegetable bouillon	

Preheat the oven to 350°F/180°C. Grease a loaf pan and line it with waxed paper. Melt the butter in a large pan over medium heat. Add the garlic and onion and cook, stirring, for 3 minutes, until softened. Remove from the heat and stir in the nuts, bread crumbs, egg, thyme, bouillon, and seasoning.

Spoon the mixture into the loaf pan and level the surface. Cook in the center of the preheated oven for 30 minutes or until cooked through and golden brown. The loaf is done when a skewer inserted into the center comes out clean. About halfway through the cooking time, make the sauce. Put all the ingredients into a pan and bring to a boil. Reduce the heat and simmer, stirring occasionally, for 15 minutes.

To serve, remove the sauce from the heat and discard the cinnamon stick. Remove the nut roast from the oven and turn out. Garnish with thyme; serve with the sauce and Brussels sprouts.

feta cheese & cranberry tarts

easy	
serves 4	
20 minutes	
15 minutes	

ingredients

4 tbsp olive oil
1 onion, chopped
8 black olives, pitted and chopped
generous ¾ cup cranberries
1 eating apple
1 tbsp lemon juice

8 sheets of phyllo pastry, cut into
16 squares measuring 5 inches/
13 cm across
4½ oz/125 g feta cheese (drained
weight), cut into small cubes

Preheat the oven to 350°F/180°C. Heat 2 tablespoons of oil in a skillet over medium heat. Add the onion and cook, stirring, for 3 minutes, until slightly softened. Remove from the heat and stir in the olives and cranberries. Core and chop the apple and add it to the pan with the lemon juice. Stir well and set aside.

Brush the phyllo squares with the remaining oil and use them to line 4 muffin pans. Place 4 sheets in each pan, staggering them so that the overhanging corners make a decorative star shape.

Divide the cranberry filling between the four tart shells. Scatter over the feta cheese and bake in the center of the preheated oven for about 10 minutes until golden. Serve hot.

herbed salmon
with hollandaise sauce

		ingredients	
easy	4 salmon fillets, about 6 oz/175 g each, skin removed	salt and pepper	
		1 cup butter, cut into small cubes	
serves 4	salt and pepper	juice of 1 lemon	
	2 tbsp olive oil		
	1 tbsp chopped fresh dill	chopped fresh chives, to garnish	
	1 tbsp chopped fresh chives		
15 minutes		TO SERVE	
	HOLLANDAISE SAUCE	freshly boiled new potatoes	
	3 egg yolks	freshly cooked snow peas	
8–10 minutes	1 tbsp water		

Preheat the broiler to medium. Rinse the fish fillets under cold running water and pat dry with paper towels. Season with salt and pepper. Combine the olive oil with the dill and chives, then brush the mixture over the fish. Transfer to the broiler and cook for about 6–8 minutes, turning once and brushing with more oil and herb mixture, until cooked to your taste.

Meanwhile, to make the sauce, put the egg yolks in a heatproof bowl over a pan of boiling water. Add the water and season with salt and pepper. Lower the heat and simmer, whisking constantly, until the mixture begins to thicken. Whisk in the butter, cube by cube, until the mixture is thick and shiny. Whisk in the lemon juice, then remove from the heat.

Remove the fish from the broiler and transfer to individual serving plates. Pour over the sauce and garnish with chopped fresh chives. Serve with freshly boiled new potatoes and snow peas.

traditional roast turkey with wine & mushrooms

		ingredients	
easy		6½–7¾ lb/3–3.5 kg oven-ready turkey 6 tbsp olive oil 1 garlic clove, finely chopped scant ½ cup red wine	2 tbsp finely chopped fresh sage 1 tbsp lemon juice salt and pepper
serves 4		STUFFING 3½ oz/100 g white mushrooms 1 onion, chopped 6 tbsp butter 1 garlic clove, chopped scant 2 cups fresh bread crumbs	PORT & CRANBERRY SAUCE ½ cup sugar 1 cup port 1¾ cups fresh cranberries
25 minutes			
3 hours 20 minutes			TO SERVE Roast Garlic Potatoes (see page 34) Spiced Winter Vegetables (see page 32)

Preheat the oven to 400°F/200°C. To make the stuffing, clean and chop the mushrooms, put them in a pan with the onion and butter and cook for 3 minutes. Remove from the heat and stir in the other ingredients. Rinse the turkey, pat dry with paper towels, fill the neck end with stuffing, and truss with string.

Pour the oil into a roasting dish and put the turkey in it. Rub the garlic over the bird and pour the wine over. Roast for 20 minutes. Baste, reduce the heat to 375°F/190°C, and roast for 40 minutes. Baste again and cover with foil. Roast for 2 hours, basting regularly. Check the bird is done by inserting a knife between the legs and body. If the juices run clear, it is done. Remove from the oven and let stand for 25 minutes. Meanwhile, put the sugar, port, and cranberries into a pan. Warm over medium heat until almost boiling. Reduce the heat, simmer for 15 minutes, stirring, then remove from the heat. Serve with the turkey and vegetables.

roast turkey asian-style

		ingredients	
	easy	6½–7¾ lb/3–3.5 kg oven-ready turkey 6 tbsp olive oil 1 tbsp lime juice	2 tbsp chopped fresh kaffir lime leaves juice of 1 lime 1 tbsp rice wine
	serves 4	STUFFING 2 scallions, trimmed and chopped 1 large garlic clove, chopped	salt and pepper TO GARNISH
	20 minutes	2 tbsp sesame oil 1 lemon grass stem, about 2¾ inches/ 7 cm long	wedges of fresh lime fresh coriander, chopped TO SERVE
	3 hours 5 minutes	1 tbsp grated fresh gingerroot 1 small red chile, seeded and chopped	freshly boiled jasmine rice freshly cooked seasonal vegetables

Preheat the oven to 400°F/200°C. To make the stuffing, cook the scallions and garlic in the sesame oil over low heat for 2 minutes. Remove from the heat and stir in the other ingredients, seasoned to taste. Rinse the turkey and pat dry with paper towels. Fill the neck end of the turkey with stuffing and truss with string.

Pour 4 tablespoons of olive oil into a large roasting dish and place the turkey in it. Mix the lime juice with the remaining oil and brush all over the turkey. Roast for 20 minutes. Baste the turkey, reduce the heat to 375°F/190°C, and roast for 40 minutes. Baste again and cover with foil. Roast for 2 hours, basting regularly. Check the bird is done by inserting a knife between the legs and body. If the juices run clear, it is done. Remove from the oven and let stand for 25 minutes. Serve the turkey with jasmine rice and seasonal vegetables, garnished with lime wedges and fresh coriander.

yuletide goose
with honey & pears

		ingredients	
easy	7¾–10 lb/3.5–4.5 kg oven-ready goose	TO SERVE	
	1 tsp salt	Roast Garlic Potatoes (see page 34)	
serves 4	4 pears	Spiced Winter Vegetables (see page 32)	
	1 tbsp lemon juice	Brussels Sprouts with Buttered	
	4 tbsp butter	Chestnuts (see page 38)	
20 minutes	2 tbsp honey	Honey-Glazed Red Cabbage with	
	lemon slices, to garnish	Golden Raisins (see page 36)	
3–3½ hours			

Preheat the oven to 425°F/220°C. Rinse the goose and pat dry. Use a fork to prick the skin all over, then rub with salt. Place the bird upside down on a rack in a roasting pan. Roast for 30 minutes. Drain off the fat. Turn the bird over and roast for 15 minutes. Drain off the fat. Reduce the heat to 350°F/180°C and roast for 15 minutes per 1 lb/450 g. Cover with foil 15 minutes before the end of the cooking time. Check the bird is done by inserting a knife between the legs and body. If the juices run clear, it is done. Remove from the oven.

Peel and halve the pears and brush with lemon juice. Melt the butter and honey in a pan over low heat, then add the pears. Cook, stirring, for 5–10 minutes, until tender. Remove from the heat, arrange the pears around the goose, and pour the sweet juices over the bird. Garnish with lemon slices and serve with garlic potatoes, winter vegetables, Brussels sprouts, and red cabbage.

sliced duck breast
with madeira & blueberries

		ingredients	
easy		6 duck breasts (skin left on) 1 garlic clove, chopped grated zest and juice of 1 orange 1 tbsp chopped fresh parsley salt and pepper	TO GARNISH blueberries orange slices
serves 4			TO SERVE roast potatoes selection of freshly cooked vegetables
15 minutes + 1 hour to marinate		MADEIRA & BLUEBERRY SAUCE 5½ oz/150 g blueberries 1 cup Madeira 1 tbsp redcurrant jelly	
15 minutes			

Use a sharp knife to make several shallow diagonal cuts in each duck breast. Put the duck in a glass bowl with the garlic, orange, and parsley. Season, and stir well. Turn the duck in the mixture until thoroughly coated. Cover with plastic wrap and place in the refrigerator to marinate for at least 1 hour.

Heat a dry, nonstick skillet over medium heat. Add the duck breasts and cook for 4 minutes, then turn them over and cook for another 4 minutes or according to taste. Remove from the heat, cover the pan, and let stand for 5 minutes.

Halfway through the cooking time, put the blueberries, Madeira, and redcurrant jelly into a separate pan. Bring to a boil. Reduce the heat and simmer for 10 minutes, then remove from the heat.

Transfer the duck to serving plates and garnish with blueberries and orange slices. Serve with roast potatoes, a selection of freshly cooked vegetables, and the Madeira and blueberry sauce.

redcurrant-glazed ham
with madeira sauce

	ingredients	
easy	4 lb 8 oz/2 kg lean ham	TO GARNISH
	4 cloves	orange slices
	6 tbsp redcurrant jelly	lemon slices
serves 4	1 tbsp whole-grain mustard	
	3 tbsp Madeira	TO SERVE
	grated zest and juice of 1 orange	Honey-Glazed Red Cabbage with
15 minutes	grated zest and juice of 1 lemon	Golden Raisins (see page 36)
		freshly cooked green beans
		freshly boiled new potatoes
2 1/2 hours		

Bring a large pan of water to a boil. Reduce the heat and add the
ham and the cloves. Cover and simmer for 1 hour, topping up the
water level when necessary.

Preheat the oven to 350°F/180°C. Remove the ham from the heat,
drain, and remove the skin. Place the meat, fat side up, on a rack
in a roasting dish. Using a sharp knife, score the fat on the ham.
Mix 2 tablespoons of redcurrant jelly with the mustard, then rub it
into the scored skin. Cook in the preheated oven for 1 1/2 hours, or
until cooked through. About 5 minutes before the end of the
cooking time, put the remaining redcurrant jelly in a small pan with
the Madeira and the citrus zest and juice. Warm gently over low
heat and simmer, stirring, for 5 minutes.

Remove the ham from the oven, transfer to serving plates, and
garnish with citrus slices. Serve with the Madeira sauce, red
cabbage, green beans, and new potatoes.

sweet & sour glazed pork

		ingredients
easy		2 lb 4 oz/1 kg pork loin, backbone removed and rind scored	3½ oz/100 g white mushrooms, chopped
serves 4		salt and pepper	scant 2 cups fresh bread crumbs
		6 tbsp honey	2 tbsp finely chopped fresh sage
		1 tbsp wine vinegar	1 tbsp lemon juice
		1 tsp soy sauce	salt and pepper
20 minutes		1 tsp Dijon mustard	
			fresh sage leaves, to garnish
		STUFFING	
1 hour 40 minutes		6 tbsp butter	TO SERVE
		1 onion, chopped	Roast Garlic Potatoes (see page 34)
			Spiced Winter Vegetables (see page 32)

Preheat the oven to 450°F/230°C. To make the stuffing, melt the butter in a pan over medium heat. Add the onion and cook, stirring, for about 3 minutes, until softened. Add the mushrooms and cook for another 2 minutes. Remove from the heat and stir in the bread crumbs, sage, lemon juice, and seasoning.

Put the stuffing in the middle of the pork loin, then roll up and tie the loin with several pieces of string. Place the joint in a roasting pan, rub the skin with plenty of salt, and season with pepper. In a small bowl, mix together the honey, vinegar, soy sauce, and mustard. Pour the mixture over the pork.

Cook in the preheated oven for 20 minutes, then reduce the heat to 350°F/180°C and cook, basting from time to time, for about 1¼ hours, or until cooked through. Remove from the oven and let stand for 15 minutes. Garnish with fresh sage leaves and serve with garlic potatoes and winter vegetables.

hazelnut crusted lamb

		ingredients	
easy		8 best end of neck lamb cutlets, excess fat removed	2 tbsp chopped fresh parsley
			2 tbsp chopped fresh thyme
serves 4		salt and pepper	6 tbsp basil oil
		6 tbsp flour	
		2 eggs, beaten	sprigs of fresh thyme, to garnish
20 minutes		3 cups fresh white or whole-wheat bread crumbs	TO SERVE
		½ cup hazelnuts, lightly toasted and chopped	Roast Garlic Potatoes (see page 34)
10 minutes			fresh salad greens

Season the lamb cutlets on both sides with salt and pepper. Put the flour on a large plate, and place the beaten eggs in a large bowl. Take another large bowl and mix together the bread crumbs, hazelnuts, and herbs. Season well.

Turn the lamb cutlets in the flour, dip them in the eggs, then coat well in the hazelnut mixture. Heat the oil in a skillet over medium heat. Add the cutlets to the pan and cook for 5 minutes, then turn them over and cook on the other side for another 5 minutes (you may need to do this in batches). Lift out of the pan and transfer to serving plates. Garnish with sprigs of thyme and serve with garlic potatoes and fresh salad greens.

festive beef wellington

		ingredients	
easy		1 lb 10 oz/750 g thick beef fillet	1 egg, beaten
		2 tbsp butter	
		salt and pepper	chopped fresh sage, to garnish
serves 4		2 tbsp vegetable oil	
		1 garlic clove, chopped	TO SERVE
		1 onion, chopped	Roast Garlic Potatoes (see page 34)
20 minutes		6 oz/175 g crimini mushrooms	Garlic Mushrooms with White Wine
		1 tbsp chopped fresh sage	and Chestnuts (see page 40)
		salt and pepper	freshly cooked Brussels sprouts
1 hour 10 minutes		12 oz/350 g frozen puff pastry dough, thawed	

Preheat the oven to 425°F/220°C. Put the beef in a roasting pan, spread with butter, and season. Roast for 30 minutes, then remove from the oven. Meanwhile, heat the oil in a pan over medium heat. Add the garlic and onion and cook, stirring, for 3 minutes. Stir in the mushrooms, sage, and seasoning, and cook for 5 minutes. Remove from the heat.

Roll out the dough into a rectangle large enough to enclose the beef, then place the beef in the middle and spread the mushroom mixture over it. Bring the long sides of the dough together over the beef and seal with beaten egg. Tuck the short ends over (trim away excess dough) and seal. Place on a cookie sheet, seam-side down. Make 2 slits in the top. Decorate with dough shapes and brush with beaten egg. Bake for 40 minutes. If it browns too quickly, cover with foil. Remove from the oven, garnish with sage, and serve with garlic potatoes, garlic mushrooms, and sprouts.

roast pheasant with red wine & herbs

easy	
serves 4	
20 minutes	
1 hour	

ingredients

scant ½ cup butter, slightly softened
1 tbsp chopped fresh thyme
1 tbsp chopped fresh parsley
2 oven-ready young pheasants
salt and pepper
4 tbsp vegetable oil
½ cup red wine

TO SERVE
Honeyed Parsnips (see page 30)
sautéed potatoes
freshly cooked Brussels sprouts

Preheat the oven to 375°F/190°C. Put the butter into a bowl and mix in the chopped herbs. Lift the skins off the pheasants, taking care not to tear them, and push the herb butter under the skins. Season with salt and pepper. Pour the oil into a roasting pan, add the pheasants, and cook in the preheated oven for 45 minutes, basting occasionally. Remove from the oven, pour over the wine, then return to the oven and cook for another 15 minutes, or until cooked through. Check each bird is done by inserting a knife between the legs and body. If the juices run clear, they are done.

Remove the pheasants from the oven, cover them with foil, and let stand for 15 minutes. Divide between individual serving plates, and serve with honeyed parsnips, sautéed potatoes, and freshly cooked Brussels sprouts.

roast venison with brandy sauce

easy	
serves 4	
15 minutes	
2 hours	

ingredients

6 tbsp vegetable oil
salt and pepper
1 saddle of fresh venison

BRANDY SAUCE
4 tbsp vegetable bouillon
1 tbsp all-purpose flour
$^3/_4$ cup brandy
scant $^1/_2$ cup heavy cream

sprigs of fresh thyme, to garnish

TO SERVE
Roast Garlic Potatoes (see page 34)
Honeyed Parsnips (see page 30)
selection of freshly cooked vegetables

Preheat the oven to 350°F/180°C. Heat 3 tablespoons of the oil in a skillet over high heat. Season the venison, then cook it in the skillet over high heat until lightly browned all over. Pour the remaining oil into a roasting pan. Add the venison, cover with foil, and roast, basting occasionally, for about 1$^1/_2$ hours or until cooked through. Remove from the oven and transfer the venison to a serving platter. Cover with foil and set aside.

To make the sauce, pour the bouillon into the roasting pan and heat it on the stove, stirring to loosen browned bits of food from the bottom. Stir in the flour and cook for 1 minute. Gradually stir in the brandy, bring to a boil, then reduce the heat and simmer, stirring, for 10–15 minutes, until the sauce has thickened a little. Remove from the heat and stir in the cream.

Garnish the venison with thyme and serve with garlic potatoes, honeyed parsnips, a selection of vegetables, and the brandy sauce.

desserts, candies & drinks

The truly spectacular desserts in this chapter are guaranteed to finish any meal with a flourish. Whether your passion is Fruit Compôte with Port & Whipped Cream, Fresh Figs & Brandy Butter, Christmas Pudding, or a hearty slice of Christmas Cake, there will be something here to tempt you. For a lighter dessert, why not try the Brandy & Orange Ice Cream? And if you can find a little room for more, try rounding off your meal with White Chocolate Truffles, Mulled Wine, or Spiced Hot Chocolate.

festive sherry trifle

		ingredients	
	easy	**FRUIT LAYER**	**CUSTARD LAYER**
		3 $\frac{1}{2}$ oz/100 g trifle sponges	6 egg yolks
		$\frac{2}{3}$ cup raspberry jelly	$\frac{1}{4}$ cup superfine sugar
	serves 4	1 cup sherry	generous 2 cups milk
		5 $\frac{1}{2}$ oz/150 g frozen raspberries,	1 tsp vanilla extract
		thawed	
	15 minutes	14 oz/400 g canned mixed fruit,	**TOPPING**
	+ 6 hours to	drained	1 $\frac{1}{4}$ cups heavy cream
	soak/chill	1 large banana, sliced	1–2 tbsp superfine sugar
	2–3 minutes		toasted mixed nuts, chopped,
			to decorate

Spread the trifle sponges with jelly, cut them into bite-size cubes, and arrange in the bottom of a large glass serving bowl. Pour over the sherry and let stand for 30 minutes.

Combine the raspberries, canned fruit, and banana, and arrange over the sponges. Cover with plastic wrap and chill for 30 minutes.

To make the custard, put the egg yolks and sugar into a bowl and whisk together. Pour the milk into a pan and warm gently over low heat. Remove from the heat, gradually stir into the egg mixture, then return the mixture to the pan and stir constantly over low heat until thickened. Do not boil. Remove from the heat, pour into a bowl, and stir in the vanilla. Cool for 1 hour. Spread the custard over the trifle, cover with plastic wrap, and chill for 2 hours.

To make the topping, whip the cream in a bowl and beat in sugar to taste. Spread over the trifle, then scatter over the nuts. Cover with plastic wrap and refrigerate for 2 hours before serving.

fruit compôte with
port & whipped cream

		ingredients	
very easy		1 tbsp butter	TOPPING
		7 oz/200 g blueberries	scant 2 cups heavy cream
serves 4		7 oz/200 g blackberries	3–4 tbsp superfine sugar
		3½ oz/100 g strawberries	
		6 tbsp port	grated chocolate, to decorate
15 minutes + 30 minutes to cool		3 tbsp blueberry jelly	
		1 tbsp cornstarch	
		1 tsp allspice	
15 minutes			

Preheat the oven to 375°F/190°C. Grease a baking dish with butter and add all the fruit.

In a bowl, mix together the port, jelly, cornstarch, and allspice. Pour the mixture over the fruit and mix well. Bake in the preheated oven for 15 minutes, stirring from time to time. Remove from the oven and let cool to room temperature, then divide between 4 decorative serving glasses.

For the topping, whip the cream in a mixing bowl and beat in sugar to taste. Spoon the mixture over the fruit, top with grated chocolate, and serve.

traditional British
christmas pudding

easy	
serves 4	
2¼ hours + 2–8 weeks to chill	
8 hours	

ingredients

1⅓ cups currants
scant 1⅓ cups raisins
scant 1¼ cups golden raisins
⅔ cup sweet sherry
¾ cup butter, plus extra
    for greasing
generous ¾ cup brown sugar
4 eggs, beaten
generous 1 cup self-rising flour

scant 2 cups fresh white or
    whole-wheat bread crumbs
⅓ cup blanched almonds, chopped
juice of 1 orange
grated zest of ½ orange
grated zest of ½ lemon
½ tsp ground allspice

holly leaves, to decorate

Put the currants, raisins, and golden raisins into a glass bowl and pour over the sherry. Let soak for at least 2 hours.

Mix the butter and sugar in a bowl. Beat in the eggs, then fold in the flour. Stir in the soaked fruit and sherry with the bread crumbs, almonds, orange juice and zest, lemon zest, and allspice. Grease an ovenproof bowl and press the mixture into it, leaving a gap of 1 inch/2.5 cm at the top. Cut a circle of waxed paper 1¼ inches/ 3 cm larger than the top of the bowl, grease with butter, and place over the pudding. Secure with string, then top with 2 layers of foil. Place the pudding in a pan filled with boiling water which reaches two-thirds of the way up the bowl. Reduce the heat and simmer for 6 hours, topping up the water when necessary.

Remove from the heat and let cool. Renew the waxed paper and foil and refrigerate for 2–8 weeks. To reheat, steam for 2 hours as before. Decorate with holly and serve.

fresh figs & brandy butter

		ingredients	
	extremely easy	½ cup butter, slightly softened	fresh mint leaves, to decorate
	serves 4	½ cup confectioners' sugar 1 tbsp brandy 12 fresh figs	
	10 minutes		
	—		

Put the butter and sugar into a small bowl and cream together well. Stir in the brandy.

Using a sharp knife, cut the figs into fourths and arrange in 4 individual serving dishes. Add a spoonful of the brandy butter, decorate with fresh mint leaves, and serve.

festive mince pies

		ingredients	
easy		scant 1½ cups all-purpose flour, plus extra for dusting	10½ oz/300 g mincemeat
		scant ½ cup butter	1 egg, beaten, for sealing and glazing
makes 12		¼ cup confectioner's sugar	confectioners' sugar, for dusting
		1 egg yolk	
20 minutes		2–3 tbsp milk	sprigs of holly, to decorate
15 minutes			

Preheat the oven to 350°F/180°C. Sift the flour into a mixing bowl. Using your fingertips, rub in the butter until the mixture resembles bread crumbs. Mix in the sugar and egg yolk. Stir in enough milk to make a soft dough, turn out onto a lightly floured counter, and knead lightly until smooth.

Shape the dough into a ball and roll out to a thickness of ½ inch/ 1 cm. Use fluted cutters to cut out 12 circles of 2¾ inches/7 cm diameter and 12 circles of 2 inches/5 cm diameter. Dust 12 tartlet pans with flour and line with the larger dough circles. Prick the bottoms with a fork, then half-fill each pie with mincemeat. Brush beaten egg around the rims, then press the smaller dough circles on top to seal. Make a small hole in the top of each one. Decorate the pies with Christmas trees made from dough trimmings. Brush all over with beaten egg, then bake for 15 minutes. Remove from the oven and cool on a wire rack. Dust with confectioners' sugar and serve.

christmas cake

	ingredients	
easy	scant 1 cup raisins	$\frac{1}{2}$ tsp salt
	generous $\frac{2}{3}$ cup pitted dates, chopped	$\frac{1}{2}$ tsp baking powder
makes one 8-inch/20-cm cake	generous $\frac{2}{3}$ cup golden raisins	1 tsp allspice
	$\frac{1}{2}$ cup candied cherries, rinsed	scant $\frac{1}{4}$ cup toasted almonds, chopped
	$\frac{2}{3}$ cup brandy	scant $\frac{1}{4}$ cup toasted hazelnuts,
45 minutes, plus 8 hours to soak	1 cup butter, plus extra for greasing	chopped
	1 cup superfine sugar	$4\frac{1}{2}$ cups confectioners' sugar
	4 eggs	1 egg white
	grated zest of 1 orange and 1 lemon	juice of 1 lemon
3 hours	1 tbsp molasses	1 tsp vanilla extract
	generous $1\frac{1}{2}$ cups all-purpose flour	holly leaves, to decorate

Make this cake at least 3 weeks in advance. Put all the fruit in a bowl, pour over the brandy, and soak overnight.

Preheat the oven to 225°F/110°C. Grease an 8-inch/20-cm cake pan and line it with waxed paper. In a bowl, cream together the butter and sugar until fluffy. Gradually beat in the eggs. Stir in the citrus zest and molasses. In a separate bowl, sift together the flour, salt, baking powder, and allspice, then fold into the egg mixture. Fold in the fruit, brandy, and nuts, then spoon into the cake pan. Bake for at least 3 hours. If it browns too quickly, cover with foil. The cake is cooked when a skewer inserted into the center comes out clean. Remove from the oven and cool on a wire rack. Store in an airtight container until required.

To make the icing, put the sugar, egg white, lemon juice, and vanilla into a bowl and mix until smooth. Spread over the cake, using a fork to give texture. Decorate with holly leaves.

brandy & orange ice cream

		ingredients	
	easy	4 egg yolks	DECORATION
		½ cup superfine sugar	finely sliced starfruit
	serves 4	generous ¾ cup milk	candied orange peel
		1 cup heavy cream	
		3 tbsp orange juice	
	25–40 minutes + 1¾–4 hours to freeze	3 tbsp brandy	
		1 tbsp finely grated orange zest	
	5 minutes		

Beat the egg yolks and sugar together in a heatproof bowl until fluffy. Put the milk, cream, orange juice, brandy, and grated orange zest into a large pan and bring to a boil. Remove from the heat and whisk into the beaten egg yolks. Return the mixture to the pan and cook, stirring constantly, over very low heat until thickened. Do not let it simmer. Remove from the heat, transfer to a bowl, and cool. Cover with plastic wrap and chill for 1 hour.

Transfer the mixture to an ice cream maker and process for 15 minutes. Alternatively, put the mixture into a freezerproof container and freeze for 1 hour. Transfer to a bowl and beat to break up the ice crystals, then put it back in the freezerproof container and freeze for 30 minutes. Repeat twice more, whisking each time and freezing for 30 minutes. Freeze until ready to serve.

To serve, soften in the refrigerator for 20 minutes beforehand. Scoop into dishes and decorate with starfruit and orange peel.

candied fruit ice cream

		ingredients	
very easy	scant $\frac{1}{2}$ cup golden raisins	$\frac{1}{2}$ cup candied cherries	
	scant $\frac{1}{2}$ cup raisins	$1\frac{3}{4}$ oz/50 g candied citrus peel	
serves 4	6 tbsp almond liqueur, such as Amaretto	$\frac{1}{2}$ cup blanched almonds, chopped	
	4 eggs, separated	strips of candied peel, to decorate	
20 minutes + 4–5 hours to freeze	$\frac{1}{2}$ cup superfine sugar		
	$2\frac{1}{2}$ cups heavy cream		
—			

Put the golden raisins and raisins into a bowl and pour over 4 tablespoons of the almond liqueur. Cover with plastic wrap and set aside to soak.

Beat the egg yolks and sugar together in a large bowl until fluffy. In a separate bowl, whisk together the cream and remaining almond liqueur, then whisk the mixture into the beaten egg yolks. In a separate bowl, whisk the egg whites until stiff peaks form, then fold into the cream mixture along with the soaked fruit, cherries, candied peel, and chopped almonds.

Transfer the mixture into a large ovenproof bowl, cover, and freeze for 4–5 hours until set. To serve, dip the bowl in hot water to loosen the ice cream, then turn it out onto a serving plate. Decorate with candied peel and serve.

white chocolate truffles

		ingredients	
easy		4¼ oz/120 g white chocolate, broken into small, even-size pieces	2 tbsp heavy cream
			½ tsp brandy
makes 20		4 tbsp butter, softened to room temperature	grated white chocolate, to decorate
15 minutes + 2½–3 hours to chill			
5 minutes			

Put the chocolate pieces into a heatproof glass bowl and place over a pan of hot but not simmering water. When it starts to melt, stir gently until completely melted. Do not overheat, or the chocolate will separate. Remove from the heat and gently stir in the butter, then the cream and brandy. Let cool, then cover with plastic wrap and refrigerate for 2–2½ hours until set.

Remove the chocolate mixture from the refrigerator. Using a teaspoon, scoop out small pieces of the mixture, then use your hands to roll them into balls. To decorate, roll the balls in grated white chocolate. To store, transfer to an airtight container and refrigerate for up to 12 days.

spiced hot chocolate

		ingredients	
very easy		7 oz/200 g semisweet chocolate (preferably one containing at least 70% cocoa solids)	grated white chocolate, to decorate
serves 4		scant 3 1/2 cups milk	
10 minutes		2 tsp sugar	
5 minutes		1 tsp ground allspice	

Break the chocolate into small, even-size pieces. Put the milk, chocolate, sugar, and allspice into a pan over medium heat. Whisk, stirring constantly, until the chocolate has melted and the mixture is simmering but not boiling.

Remove from the heat and pour into heatproof glasses. Sprinkle over some grated white chocolate and serve.

mulled wine

		ingredients	
extremely easy		3 cups red wine	½ tsp ground allspice
		3 tbsp sherry	2 tbsp clear honey
serves 4		8 cloves	1 seedless orange, cut into wedges
		1 cinnamon stick	1 lemon, cut into wedges
5–10 minutes			
5–10 minutes			

Put the wine, sherry, cloves, cinnamon, allspice, and honey into a pan and stir together well. Warm over low heat, stirring, until just starting to simmer, but do not let it boil. Remove from the heat and pour through a strainer. Discard the cloves and cinnamon stick.

Return the wine to the pan with the orange and lemon wedges. Warm gently over very low heat, but do not let it boil. Remove from the heat, pour into heatproof glasses, and serve hot.

christmas punch

		ingredients	
	extremely easy	4 cups red wine	scant ½ cup orange liqueur, such as
		4 tbsp sugar	Cointreau
	serves 10	1 cinnamon stick	2 seedless oranges, cut into wedges
		1¾ cups boiling water	2 dessert apples, cored and cut
		scant ½ cup brandy	into wedges
	10 minutes	scant ½ cup sherry	
	5–10 minutes		

Put the wine, sugar, and cinnamon into a large pan and stir together well. Warm over low heat, stirring, until just starting to simmer, but do not let it boil. Remove from the heat and pour through a strainer. Discard the cinnamon stick.

Return the wine to the pan and stir in the water, brandy, sherry, and orange liqueur. Add the orange and apple wedges and warm gently over very low heat, but do not let it boil. Remove from the heat and pour into a large, heatproof punch-bowl. Ladle into heatproof glasses and serve hot.

index